The Content Marketing Playbook Strategies to Attract the Right Customers

Author: Adella Pasos

Are you Interested in learning how content marketing can improve your business and profits? Tired of getting nowhere fast? The content marketing playbook is a strategic guide that explains how to source, produce, organize, distribute and promote valuable content that attracts new customers.

This book is perfect for anyone who wants to sell products or services, anyone who works in marketing, sales or management and is interested in learning how to acquire more customers. Content marketing will specifically address your customers problems, provide them with your solution and become a source of revenue that you can rely on.

If you want to learn everything you'll ever need to know about content marketing, this is the book for you!

The Content Marketing Playbook
Strategies to Attract the Right Customers

Published by Adella Pasos

Copyright © 2020 www.adellapasos.com

Table of Contents

Introduction: About This Book

Chapter 1: Content Marketing Basics

This chapter discusses the importance of content marketing is, reveals companies that are actively using content marketing, ways to make content marketing work for you and where to start.

Chapter 2: Ways to Get Content Ideas

This chapter will outline how to recognize the right idea and ways to find a good idea that provides value for each type of customer you have.

Chapter 3: How Much Content Do You Actually Need?

When you are on a budget, sometimes you can't afford to become a content powerhouse right at the start. This chapter will help you figure out how much content to invest your time and money in.

Chapter 4: List of Popular Content Types

Choosing content should be based upon how your target audience consumes media online. Learn the 15 most popular content types.

Chapter 5: Places to Get Content Created on a Budget

This chapter explains exactly where to get quality content for less. You don't need a big budget to get the content created that matters the most.

Table of Contents Continued...

Chapter 6: Ways to Distribute Content Everywhere

How do you plan to get in front of your prospects? This chapter will cover all the methods used to promote your content.

Chapter 7: How to Make Money From Your Content

If you are using content to drive traffic to your website for entertainment or educational purposes, but not necessarily to make a sale or collect a lead, this chapter will go over strategies like paywalls, affiliate linking, freemium and membership monetization models.

Chapter 8: Top Recommended Content Marketing Platforms

Confused on what platform you need to product, organize and distribute your content? This chapter recommends a few platforms that will get you set up in the right direction.

Chapter 9: Content Marketing Resources

This chapter includes a list of impressive content marketing templates and systems for various niches. So you can design beautiful content campaigns to effectively communicate with your audience and share your message.

Appendix: Frequently Asked Questions

This is a great spot to check out the most common questions people have about other ways to make money and benefits of content marketing.

Introduction: About This E-Book

Hello! and thanks for downloading this awesome book. Throughout the course of this book you will learn how to create, promote and profit from content marketing. I wrote this book for you to truly see that your business can succeed with a great content marketing strategy.

The strategies that I've listed in the book will explain how you can get paid from using content marketing, as well as where and how to get started. Entrepreneurs, start-ups, and even large fortune 500 companies are using the same strategies to gain millions of dollars. So, where's your piece of the pie? Who doesn't love a fast track to success?

Who am I?

I am an International Business Coach and Marketing Strategist who has shared my passion for growing brands from the ground up. I've worked with startups, small businesses, global corporations and entertainment talent that recognize the value of marketing. I give my clients the ability to sell more by preparing them with the right strategies in social media, mobile, merchandising, and events. Providing simple solutions to complex challenges, I've placed all that I know into these books.

Now, it's time for you to apply the knowledge, and get out there and put your game face on!

Cheers to your success,

Adella Pasos

Chapter 1: Content Marketing Basics

Why Content Marketing?

Content is King! I'm sure you've heard that phrase many times before. But really, what does that mean? Content marketing is a strategy used by small and big companies alike. They basically create, distribute and promote content to their target customer in order to bring in new traffic and leads to the business.

The use of content marketing is very important when you are looking to target those customers who are "searching" for answers to their problems. When compared to Paid Marketing, Content marketing is proven to generate up to 3x more leads. It's also a fact that businesses who publish 16 or more posts per month get on average 3.5x more traffic than those who only publish 0-4 per month.

FACT: 47% of business to business buyers will read 3-5 pieces of content before engaging with a sales person. Once convinced, they will inquire or call for more information to purchase. Having as much information out there as possible can only benefit you and your business.

How Event Marketing Helps

- Increase Sales Generate Leads
- Convey Your Message
- Send Traffic to Your Website
- Get More Appointments &
- Bookings Collect Feedback & Insights
- Create New Streams of Income

What are the Benefits of Content Marketing?

If your brand is having a hard time reaching a target audience, or generating traffic and sales, content marketing has a big advantage over many other strategies. It will open up conversations that allow your supporters to share your valuable message.

The main benefits are:

- Increases brand visibility on search engines & social media
- Helps establish and develop relationships with your audience
- Creates loyalty and trust for your brand
- Positions you as an expert in your industry
- Opens up an opportunity to sell products and services

How Do I Start?

Step 1: Establish Your Content Strategy

The first step is deciding on the main goal of your content. It can be multiple goals for example: to collect leads, to sell, to help decision makers remember you, to collect feedback from customers, etc. A good place to start is to define at least 3-5 specific goals.

Step 2: Start Developing the Content

The next step is to 'brand' your content. All content needs to be professionally designed so that it is memorable and specific to meet your goals. I prefer to use 99designs, they have been proven the most reliable for marketing design work.

Step 3: Organize the Content Assets and Choose a Schedule

After you've got your content designed, next you'll need to organize them into 'content buckets'. Be very specific and prepared to group them by topic, type and when you'd like this content to go live. I would recommend using project management software or content management systems to keep track of the content and scheduling.

Step 4: Pick Distribution Channels

After you've prepared your content and it's organized, decide which channels you'd like to use. This could be Facebook, LinkedIn, Twitter, and YouTube, Snapchat, blogs, email list, direct mail, website articles, tv, a print publication, etc. You don't need to limit yourself to one single channel. The more, the better!

Step 5: Start Promoting the Content

There are many methods to promote your content, but the first thing you need to do is make your content visible online. When you promote, make sure your ads and promotions are exposed in places where your target market is.

You can choose to promote your content organically (the free method) or set up paid ads to drive much more traffic, quickly.

Banner, video and text ads should be posted on your audience's favorite blogs, magazines, news sites, public places and more. Don't forget about social media and using influencers to help spread via word of mouth, too! These people can and will easily amplify your content and reach

How Do I Get Paid?

Most businesses start content marketing so that they can generate leads, increase sales, look like the leader in the market, educate prospects and to increase brand awareness. The content you create should be free, of high value, 100% audience-focused. Use the content as a magnet to attract your target audience and prospects.

Here's a list of ways to make money from your content:

- Write blog posts that include links to buy your products and services
- Repurpose your blogs packaged into a paid course
- Repurpose your blogs and sell them as printed or e-books
- Add links to buy your products or services at the end of your videos
- Sell subscriptions or membership to access your premium videos
- Sell subscriptions or memberships to access your premium articles
- Sell advertising space or sponsorships on any of your content
- Giveaway a free guide and add links to buy your products and services in it
- Place a lead generation form at the end of your blogs, collect leads and send them links to buy your products and services
- Lock your content behind a paywall and sell a one-time or monthly pass for access
- Include your entire website and video assets on an ad network and get paid when people click on ads.
- Write paid reviews on complementary products and services
- Charge for pay-per-view access to an online event, webinar or video
- Accept tips and donations for your content creation efforts

Content Marketing Best Practices

Here is a list of key things to remember that will help you along the way.

1) Set realistic goals & budgets

Be specific when deciding on a goal and budget. Choose a flat number and move forward to start on content creation. You can always increase the marketing efforts once you have a plan and budget in place. Once you know your budget, start setting up the marketing goals. Setting up a content strategy breaks down to asking yourself a few key questions:

- How many people do I want or need to reach?
- How much time do I have to reach them?
- What do we need to get this done?
- What channel would best suit this type of content?
- Do I currently have the abilities or resources to make this happen?
- Is my goal to sell products, obtain signups, educate or entertain?

2) Create Titles & Choose Topics That Attract

A good title will go a long way. Besides, most people will click your link because they are curious and may be speculating finally finding a solution to their answer. Since so many people are creating content every day, you'll need to be able to stand out. Having an attractive and descriptive title will help you achieve balance and increase clicks.

3) Double check all content for clarity and simplicity

People don't have much time and are always in a hurry nowadays. No one has time to pick through and piece together your content. If you can describe what you are selling or promoting with clarity, you'll get more leads and sales. Try to break things down in a simple way. Use short paragraphs and add things like bullet points.

4) Use a mix of videos and images

You want to get as much buy-in as possible and increase viewership. Pictures and videos provide more value and are far more attractive than just words. Make sure to use a good even ratio of words to images. Images will penetrate the mind, people remember what they saw more than what they've read. It's best practice to include high quality, attractive images. You can buy stock photos and videos on PhotoDune for an affordable price.

Chapter 2: Ways to Get Content Ideas

1. Q&A Forums (Quora, Yahoo! Answers, etc.)

One of the main places to go for content inspiration is Quora. Quora is a place to gain and share knowledge. It's a platform to ask questions and connect with people who contribute unique insights and quality answers. There you will find tons of customers waiting for answers and solutions.

2. Industry-Specific Forums (Your Readers' Forums)

If you own a business in construction for example, simply google "construction + forums" and a list of websites will come up with people who chat online, share news and ask questions. This will give you a good idea of what people in your niche are looking for.

3. Online Groups (Facebook, LinkedIn, Reddit)

Many of the major social networks now have niche groups. Join in on the conversation and find groups that are interested in what you have to sell. You'll find people looking for solutions and your content should be able to provide answers for them.

4. Industry Publications: Popular Titles and Topics

If you type in "Tech News" or "Healthcare News" or "Finance News", you'll find sites in your industry that publish the latest trends, tips and more. Look for articles with high engagement, meaning they have good comments, shares and likes and re-create your own branded content from that information.

5. Social Media: Hashtags

Use social media to your benefit! You can find your ideal followers by simply following the hashtags that are relevant to your industry and viewing what articles are being published, what buzzwords are popular and what type of questions are being asked. This will lead to potential topics for your own content.

6. Google Search Box & Related Suggestions

Have you ever noticed that suggestions automatically appear when you start typing in the google search box? Also at the bottom of the search result pages, it will show you searches that relate and can clue you in on what topics to cover in your own content.

7. Topic Generator

These website's will generate popular titles for you to use depending on your industry's terms and keywords.

- Hubspot's Blog Topic
- Generator Portent's Content Idea Generator
- SEOPressor Blog TItle Generator

8. Use BuzzSumo

This tool allows you to see which content has the best social media performance. Just type in any domain name and you'll get a list of their top performing content.

9. Use a Keyword & Content Finder Tool

Use this website semrush.com to search for a common industry topic keyword. It will give you not only the top performing websites and backlink to their content, but also show you questions related to those keywords that people are asking and show you how high they rank.

10. Use Google Trends

Use the google trends website to find topics people are searching for that correlate with your keywords, industry or niche. You'd be surprised at some of the topics that correlate. This is a good tool to give you more content generating ideas.

Chapter 3: How Much Content Do You Actually Need?

When you are on a budget, sometimes you can't afford to become a content powerhouse right at the start. How much content do you actually need? First you need to decide how many types of buyers you have for your products and services? and what industries are they in?

This will lay the groundwork for what type of questions they may have and how you can provide an answer and a solution. Let's say you cater to small businesses, midsize and large enterprises. You'll then need 3 personas.

Next, map out how many buying stages you have for each. Some sales cycles are longer than others in certain industries, so for the sake of time, let's assume 4 stages. Now, let's say you want to answer 5 questions for each stage per persona. You have 3 x 4 x 5 = 60 pieces of content that is needed to start.

These types of content can be in the format of blog posts, videos, webinars, ebooks, you name it. Do you research and make a decision on what to write or record and promote it to your target audience.

Using this simple formula (# of personas x #of stages in buyers cycle x #of questions to be answered) = How much content you need. Will help you get started on the right path quickly.

Chapter 4: List of Popular Content Types

Don't just pick one type of content. Choose from many.You should be making content for each stage of the buyers path. Some people are looking, some are only browsing, some are in the consideration stage and others are ready to buy and take action.

I would highly recommend that the "ready to buy stage" is where you spend most of your time on content creation. I would recommend you always always always have a lead generator at the end of each piece of contact just in case those who are readying, watching or listening decide to buy or simply opt-in for more information. Always map the content to the customer's pain point.

Here are some content types that lead to sales by stage:

(Only Looking) - No Risk Content: Blog Posts, Youtube Videos, Podcasts, Interviews, Audio Files, Market Trend Reports, Charts and Graphs

(Browsing for more information) - Low Risk Offer: E-books, Templates, Reports, White Papers, Guides, Resource Lists

(Consideration State) - Comparison Content: Social Media, Testimonials, FAQs, Demos, Guarantees, Trials, Webinars, Newsletters, Endorsements, Webinars, Reviews & Past Customer Positive Feedback

(Ready to Buy) - BUY ACTION: Contact Us buttons, Quote Page, Buy Now / Add to Cart Product & Service Pages, Sales Inquiry Pages, Request Pricing Page

Here's a list of content ideas that people love

- To be in the know about a specific topic
- Helpful tips or knowledge that helps them grow
- The latest updates in a certain industry or on a topic
- Inspiring stories or visuals
- Stories of people achieving greatness
- Ideas on how to live a healthier life
- Stories and tales from the well travelled or experienced people
- Opinions and sharing what's on your mind
- Answers to burning or popular questions
- List of "Best and Worst' videos / blog posts
- Review videos and blog posts
- Exposing secrets of an industry or topic
- Before and Afters
- Show and Tell
- Transformations
- New findings and Research Studies
- Quick advice for people on the go
- List of ways to do something or complete an activity
- Lists of places to find something
- This vs That videos
- Competitions or Challenges
- Panel or round table discussions
- Content that helps your audience advance, build or enhance
- List of Your 'Favorite" or "Top Recommended" things

- Reunions or reuniting with something or someone lost
- Here's my journey videos and blogs
- Videos on people who beat the odds or have a special talent
- Going back in time videos - revisiting certain decades
- Revealing or uncovering big mistakes
- Surprising a family member, friend, co-worker or spouse
- Are you paying too much videos
- Acts of goodwill videos and posts
- Announcement of new features to products or services
- Business expansion videos - before and after
- Exposing Myth videos
- Hot Topic Videos: Facts vs Opinions
- Overcoming adversity videos
- New uses for old product videos
- Solving a common problem videos
- Personal Success Story Videos
- Interviews
- Surprising fact videos
- Prank videos
- Methods, ways or strategies to connect, restore, find, repair, prepare or maintain something

Creating Content By User's Search Intent

If you are targeting users who search online, you'll want to create content that is directly related to the user's intent. This will increase your likelihood of connecting with the customer and provide the value of what they are looking for which in turn can equal increased sales.

First, most people searching online are looking to "Know" something, "Do" something, visit a particular website, or locate a store or visit a place in person. Remember the longer the query, the more specific and more clear the user intent becomes.

Example: If someone enters *"how to get rid of my babies foot wart"* or *"how to best make use of old high heels".*

These are really specific questions they have. Creating content that provides an answer and a solution is your key in the door to making sales if you have a product or service that aligns with the customer's intent. Broad search terms don't have much intent behind them, for example *"camera, digital cameras, most expensive camera",* more specific terms like *"affordable camera, or black digital SLR camera, or even "Canon EOS mark 5",* these types of searches show the user is intending to decide on a specific item **and possibly make a transaction.**

The Intent to "Know" - Informational

Targeting people who are looking to know or learn something will type in questions like this into the search bar: *"How many calories in a banana?",* *"How tall is Obama", "how many grams is a pound?"* or "how many people own Maserati's?" "what are Macy's gift wrapping options?", "who won the Australian open 2019?, "most expensive steak in the world", "how to treat a chronic cold". These types of questions indicate that the person is interested in content that answers their specific question.

Most answers are simple, but sometimes can be complex or do not just have a short answer. Many times people searching in the "know" category are not ready to purchase anything, they are just strictly looking for a quick answer. This is the research phase of the buyer's journey.

The Intent to "Go" - Navigational

Targeting people looking to go means they are looking to visit a specific website or find a location nearby. People will type in queries like "nearest chinese restaurant" or "walmart hours" or "best sushi near me". This is sometimes the post-sales stage of the buyer's journey. True navigational queries have very clear intent – the person searching has an exact website in mind and if you're not that site, you're content or ads may not be relevant to their needs.

NOTE: It's important to make sure your own brand's information is readily available and found at the top spot when people search for your brand or company's name.

The Intent to "Do" - Transactional

Targeting people looking to do something means they are trying to complete a specific goal or activity. Which is usually to purchase something as a solution.They want to buy, download, obtain, or interact with something.

For example: If the user types in *"download candy crush"*, *"what is my bmi"*, *"calculate my credit score"*, *"buy Spider-man on dvd"*, *"buy newest toshiba camera"*, *"buy cheap sneakers"*, *"get insurance quotes"*. This is the comparison phase and sometimes can indicate the buyer is in the decision stage of the journey.

Mapping User Intent to Buyers Journey Example

Here's a clean example of how the user intent and buyers journey work together as one:

Problem Recognition - User realizes she needs to shave and intends to **"Go"** search for a solution near her.

Research Phase - User searches for *"the best way to shave my legs"* and searches *"laser hair removal reviews"* and *"benefits of laser hair removal"*. She "intends to **"Know"** something. Your content should either be at the top spot organically or be placed in a paid ad when the user has searched for those terms.

Comparison - User found your website through content marketing which provides answers on the methods to get rid of hair and now compares different offers and options on your website. At this point, she intends to **"Do"** something.

Decision - User decided to purchase a laser hair removal package because you had great content, catered to her stage in the decision making process and had a discount offer to save $50 off for buying today.

Content Types By Buyer's Journey

FOR PROBLEM RECOGNITION & RESEARCH STAGE

Blog Posts - Tips & Advice Industry

Related White Paper Free

How-to-eBook

How-to-Videos Educational

Webinar Infographics

Infographics

Video Course or Tutorial

Opinion Blog Post

FAQ and Q&A Videos

Digital PDF Guide

Templates or Plans

FOR COMPARISON & DECISION STAGE

Catalogs Pricing Sheets

Case Studies / Reviews

Live Demo / Webinar

Product Spec Sheets

Comparison Sheet

Free Estimate or Quote

Video, Survey or Quiz

Trial Offer or Download

Review Video

Worksheets

Chapter 5: Places to Get Content Created on a Budget

This is the way you can produce content consistently. Most audiences consume information in many different ways: Text, Videos, Podcasts, Graphics, etc. To reach as many people as you can you'll need to generate content in different ways, Now that you have a general understanding of what kind of content you need.

You'll need to get it created. Many people opt to create content on their own, but for those who don't have the time or talent. We use freelancers or agencies to create highly engaging, creative branded content to boost your marketing campaigns. You can hire people who do photography, video creation, infographic design, blog copywriters and more. Many agencies do full service, meaning they will help you go from concept through production and delivery.

After you get the content back, you'll want to plan out an editorial calendar. This will communicate when each post, video, or content should get sent or received and what time / date it's expected to be published.

Hiring and Agency vs Freelancer

Cost - As you know many agencies will charge you a large flat fee for content or a retainer to keep you on-board as a client. Freelancers are typically less expensive and will charge by the hour. Sometimes rates are even negotiable, depending on your project's budget.

Agencies however, may charge a flat monthly fee or include costs for planning, strategy and promotion. If you were just looking for a few pieces, that means you will end up paying for extra services you may not necessarily need.

Time - Freelancers are usually available fast and can be hired fairly quickly. They will be your best bet if you need a short-term project completed fast. Agencies typically have a team of people who get involved in the entire strategy and planning process, which makes getting your campaign to market slower. The benefit of this is your campaign will be well reviewed for accuracy and you'll be set up for success.

Range of Services - Most freelancers don't offer a breadth of services. It's very common to simply find a freelancer that only does graphics, or only copywriting, or only social media. Agencies usually serve as a one-stop-stop for all services from marketings strategy to web design, public relations and more.

List of Ways to Get Content Created

Don't forget content marketing is a long-term strategy, not a one-time campaign. Prepare a list of potential content types that you will need, start researching local businesses that can accommodate this request. Reach out via phone and email to gauge interest and pricing for your project.

Google - Type in *"content creation agency"* or *"content creation services"* in your google search to locate local businesses that can help you.

Google - If you are looking for something more specific type in *"marketing strategy agency"* or *"copywriters", or "hire a blog writer".*

Upwork.com - Seek out the right person from the start. You can find thousands of freelancers ready to work on your project. Filter by their expertise and skill set. Prices will vary by the hour.

Fiverr.com - Most services start at $5, but pay attention to the freelancers quality rating score and don't forget to read the reviews.

Freelancer.com - Similar to Upwork, but also includes web design, IT, Writing for Sales & Marketing.

Envato - If you don't want to make a great investment into visual content, but want affordable images to use. Check out this site.

Izea - This is a great website if you want to get influencers involved in creating content for you. Plans are really affordable to get started.

Hire Staff - You can always hire full time or part-time staff. Place your listings on a job board online to track applicants. Interview and hire someone to create content for you.

Scripted.com - This website you can quickly outsource writing for a good price and they have expert academic writers on staff.

GreatContent.com - They offer multilingual content writing with no hidden fees.

Chapter 6: Ways to Distribute
Content Everywhere

Now you have your content and you are ready to go, how do you get it in front of your prospects? Let's go over all the methods used to get the word out there and promote your content. These are the list of PAID content promotions.

1)   Use a content promotion agency - Izea.com is a website where you can pay influencers to publish your content to their networks and be seen by their audience. Prices are very reasonable. They are required to keep the content live for up to 45 days, after that they have the right to remove it off their website or social media network.

2)   Content Discovery Networks - Websites like taboola, outbrain, revcontent, and adblade will recommend your content at the bottom of thousands of websites online. These essentially are "sponsored ads" They drive traffic to your website and launch a campaign for as low as $10.

3)   Media Buying websites - You can buy banner ads and placements with networks who will promote your e-books, videos, free white papers and more. BuySellAds.com is a great network to start minimum is around $25-50 to buy media ads.

4)   PR Newswire - You can distribute your content via a news distribution network.

5)   Facebook / Instagram Ads / Youtube / Twitter - These social networks will promote you to their users depending on the targeting and demographics you choose. Prices range and are usually cpc (cost - per-click) or cpm (cost per 1000 views).

6)   Google Adwords - Google will display your ads to promote your content in google search, in gmail, on blogs and news sites and more. Immediate promotion, easy to scale and control but can be very pricey.

7)   Buy Solo Ads - Depending on your niche, you can buy individual ads with high traffic blogs, websites who sell one off email marketing blasts. As long as your offer is relevant to their audience and offers value, they will send your content out to their entire list. You'll need to contact them asking for pricing for a solo ad.

These are the list of FREE content promotion, you won't pay for advertising, but you will use your time to get the job done.

1)   Add a web notification extension / plugin to your website - Every visitor will get asked to accept your content promotions through their internet browser. Every time you post something new, they will get an update automatically to click the link.

2)   Ask partners or friends to share your content - Get their advice on your new content and ask if they can help you promote or share your link into their network.

3)   Mention influencers in your post - tag the influencer and ask them to share their thoughts. This post could be a nomination or maybe you are telling your network about how they set a great example within your niche.

4)   Use Hashtags - For extra discovery power, use hashtags on all of your social media posts. This will help extend your reach, even outside of your own network.

5)   Engage with Online Communities - Get out there! Answer questions on Facebook Groups, Quora, Yahoo Answers, or Reddit. Talk with people who are voicing their problems and opinions. Always share helpful and relevant info and a link to your latest content or website.

6)   Schedule your content to be promoted on social media - Post Daily! Use Buffer.com to simplify and automate the posting of your content. This software allows you to connect and manage all your profiles in one central dashboard.

7)   Forum Boards - go to google and type in your "keyword" + "forum"

or "keyword" + "forums". It will yield forum boards in your niche that you can participate in conversation and share your content easily!

8)   Post on Content Curation Platform - Scoop.it, Flipboard, and Curata are places where people collect their favorite content across the web and share it.

They post around topics such as science, politics, sports, entertainment, celebrity news, viral internet stories and more. It's important to get your content on these platforms so that people can discover, share and repost for free.

9)   Email Marketing - Collect a list of people who are interested in getting you content and start publishing it to them on a weekly basis.

Chapter 7: How to Make Money From Your Content

If you are using content publishing to drive traffic to your website for entertainment or educational purposes, but not necessarily to make a sale or collect a lead, this chapter will go over strategies like paywalls, affiliate linking, freemium and membership monetization models.

First you'll need to create a money page (*a page that will ultimately sell your products or services or present an offer)*. This can range from blog posts that have recommended affiliate products or products you make for sale, it could be a landing page with a sales offer or promotion, it could be a video on page that has a "buy now" link, etc. There are a few simple ways you can engage with your audience, promote and make money through your content. **Try the following:**

Create a FB, Instagram and Twitter account - promote your own branded content organically or paid send traffic back to your money page.

Get involved with social media influencers - promote your content through their network, sending the traffic back to your money page.

Connect with partners - promote your content through their networks - organically or paid send traffic back to your money page.

Do Social Media Lead Generation and promote your content to send traffic back to your money page.

Include affiliate or buy now links on all of your blog posts, inside of e-books, pdfs, white papers.

Include paywalls on your content - people have to register for a membership or pay a flat fee to view your videos, download or read your blog content

You can give away some of your content for free, but for upgraded or exclusive content charge a fee. This is the freemium model.

You can charge other brands to "sponsor content" that you will write that offers value to your website and promotes their product as a solution.

You can create tutorial videos or product reviews and get paid by brands to create that content

You can sell your services through your content by simply including a link to your pricing page or buy now button

You can write on your blog and include Google Adsense to appear on the bottom and sides of every page. You'll get paid every time someone clicks an ad on your content

You can sell direct pages or slots to brands on your website.

For example: if you own *momslaundrytips.com*, you can create a page like *momslaundrytips.com/clorox* or *momslaundrytips.com/brandnamehere* and sell them advertising space on your website if you are a high traffic site, many brands would be interested in this. Try terms like monthly, quarterly or yearly page rental.

Work with Google: *"blog content networks"* monetization ad networks" to sign up as a "publisher" to gain access to their monetization tools. You can opt in for on-page banner ads, pre- roll video ads, display ads, interactive ads, native ads, interstitial ads and more. You get paid every time ads are shown on your content and people click.

Chapter 8: Top Recommended Content Marketing Platforms

Hubspot - This tool is for companies looking for an all-in-one marketing automation tool. This software covers email marketing, social media, and quick deploy landing pages for capturing leads. You can follow your customers through a funnel and ensure they are receiving your messages. The price range is $50-$3,200/mo+. Must call or email for demo.

Keap - The perfect marketing tool for small and midsize businesses looking to manage automated email marketing and looking to close more deals in less time. Price is $199/mo+. Must call or email for demo.

Marketo - marketing automation platform focused on account-based marketing, including email, mobile, social, digital ads, web management and analytics. Prices range from $895/mo+. Must call for a demo.

Pardot - Owned by Salesforce, it helps marketers create more leads, generate more pipeline, and empower sales to close more deals. Prices are close to $1250/mo+. Call for a demo.

Curata - Curate large volumes of content and manage marketing team workflow. Discover the best content with our self-learning engine . Easily organize and contextualize with just a few clicks. Publish and promote your content anytime and anywhere. Prices range from $499-$1000/mo +.

Chapter 9: Content Marketing Resources

<u>Theme Forest</u> - This website has the best website templates to get you started. They are easy to use and edit. They even sell a service that can help you customize the templates.

Here's a List of Useful Templates by style:

<u>Blog and Magazines under $100</u>

<u>Landing Pages under $50</u>

<u>Email Marketing Templates</u>

<u>Fiverr</u> - This website has plenty of freelancers that will help you organize, and promote your content.

Here's a List of Useful Content Gigs:

<u>Content Marketing</u> - <u>General</u>

<u>Content Writers</u>

<u>Content Strategy</u>

Appendix: "Event Marketing FAQs"

Q: Why do I need content marketing in the first place?

A: Content marketing is a great way for small businesses to generate awareness, engagement and leads which can potentially turn into sales. Good content marketing builds trust.

Q: Can I still do content marketing along with sales promotions and traditional marketing strategies?

A: Absolutely, content marketing should be coupled alongside any other marketing activities that you have going on. It's okay to promote your informational content but also promote a direct sale offer via print, tv, trade shows, etc. It is highly encouraged.

Q: What can a small business do to increase its impact on google?

A: Since there are so many companies all over the world producing hundreds of articles and videos daily, it is very hard to compete in the search engines. However, one thing you can do is target your content by niche or by industry. These people are looking to solve a particular problem that is specific.

For instance, a search term would be *"how to sell online for fashion retailers"* or *"10 ways to get more construction clients".* This will help narrow the playing field and allow you to be found faster and easier online.

Appendix: "Event Marketing FAQs"

Q: Can I build a blog on a free platform ?

A: Yes you can but there are a few limitations that you need to be aware of. First, your content is housed by the platform that you choose, so if those companies go out of business or decide to shut down, all the money and time you've invested in content, goes down the drain, too. If your content breaks their terms of service, they will also suspend your account and it will all be removed from the internet.

Q: What type of content works well for all industries?

A: Many small and large companies start with blog content. Later diving into video content on youtube, infographics, presentations on Slideshare and podcasts on iTunes.

Q: Do we have to keep creating new content?

A: Yes, you are going to want to always create new content, but you can also repurpose the same content in multiple ways. If you write a few blog posts, you can repackage them as a free e-course or as a book to send to your email subscribers. You can also turn your books into a podcast.

Appendix B: Recommended Resources

Email Marketing - Aweber

The world's best email marketing software for content marketing newsletters and auto-responders! Create emails with style and get more messages delivered fast! Create professional and powerful email marketing today.

<u>Get a Free Trial of Aweber for Content Marketing</u>

Web Hosting - Bluehost

I highly recommend using Bluehost for your website. They have an incredibly easy to use 1-click automatic word press installation and amazing customer service. The link below gets you a special discount off the regular price!

<u>Get a 30 Day Money Back Guarantee for a New Website</u>

Business Incorporation - MyCorporation

Everything you need to start, maintain and protect your business. Easily form a corporation or Limited Liability Company in no time. Learn which entity is best for your business!

<u>Legally Incorporate Your Business Today</u>

Appendix B: Recommended Resources

Business Supply Purchases - Amazon Business

Create a free Amazon Business account to save time and money on business purchases with competitive B2B prices and discounts. Satisfy your sourcing requirements and get Tax-exempt purchasing.

Get Discounted Supplies with Amazon for Business

Content Marketing Materials - 99designs

I've always trusted them with creating online graphics, logos and website designs. You can use them for all sorts of projects like packaging, email marketing designs, banner ads, business cards, trade show material and more.

Get Content Marketing Materials Designed Today

Credit Card & Payment Processing - Square

Square helps millions of event companies run their business from secure credit card processing to point of sale solutions. Get paid faster with Square. Sign up today!

Signup for Square for Business

About the Author

MARKETING EXPERT | BRAND STRATEGIST | BUSINESS COACH | TV HOST

This Business Coach and Marketing Expert has shared her passion for growing brands from the ground up. She's worked with Startups, Small Businesses, Fortune 500 Corporations and entertainment talent that recognize the value of marketing. She gives her clients the ability to access their niche market via online, social media, mobile, merchandising, and events.

The What's Your Game Plan Show features free expert advice and growth strategies for Business Owners and Executives across the globe.

Access thousands of FREE Tips, Trends and Tools to Move Your Business Forward! Contact the author:

AdellaPasos.com
Subscribe to Business Strategy TV Youtube